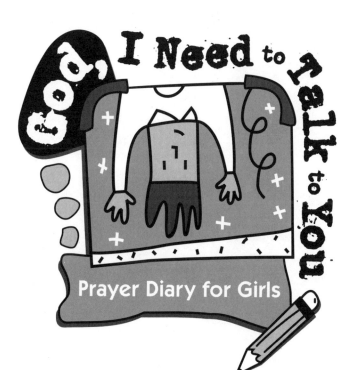

God, I Need to Talk to You

Prayer Diary for Girls

Marlene
Bagnull

SAINT LOUIS

The poems on pages 10, 14, 26, 30, 36, 38, 62, 68, 72, 80, 84, 88, 90, and 94 originally appeared in *I Am Special: Prayer Diary for Junior High Girls,* copyright © 1987 Marlene Bagnull, published by Judson Press, Valley Forge, PA.

Scripture quotations, unless otherwise indicated, are taken from THE LIVING BIBLE, © 1971 by Tyndale House Publishers, Wheaton, IL. Used by permission.

Scripture quotations marked NIV are taken from the HOLY BIBLE, NEW INTERNATIONAL VERSION®. NIV®. Copyright © 1973, 1978, 1984 by International Bible Society. Used by permission of Zondervan Publishing House. All rights reserved.

Copyright © 1997 Marlene Bagnull
Published by Concordia Publishing House
3558 S. Jefferson Avenue, St. Louis, MO 63118–3968
Manufactured in the United States of America

Library of Congress Cataloging-in-Publication Data

Bagnull, Marlene.
   God, I need to talk to you : prayer diary for girls / Marlene Bagnull.
      p.   cm.
   ISBN 0-570-04982-2
   1. Girls–Prayer-books and devotions–English.   2. Teenage girls–
Prayer-books and devotions–English.   I. Title.
BV4860.B33 1997
242' .62–dc21

                                                    97-6307

2 3 4 5 6 7 8 9 10   06 05 04 03 02 01 00 99 98 97

Contents

As You Begin

Imagine how excited you would be if someone gave you the most beautifully wrapped gift you had ever seen. The paper glimmers and sparkles like a thousand stars. The ribbon and bow are made of luscious velvet and are your favorite color. Surely the gift inside must be fabulous! But what if you decided never to unwrap the package? Wouldn't the person who gave you the gift feel really sad?

Well, there's nothing imaginary about the gift of prayer our heavenly Father has given us. It's a priceless gift, but it's a gift we need to unwrap and open. In His Word, God invites us to talk to Him about anything and everything that's on our mind. You see, He really cares about us! And He doesn't just listen to our prayers, He answers them in wonderful ways.

This prayer diary will help you learn more about God and about prayer. You can write your own prayers in this book or in a separate notebook. And what's really exciting is going back and seeing how God has answered your prayers.

You might want to skip around in this book and find prayers that speak about things that are happening in your life right now. No matter how you use this book, I know that God will hear your prayers and answer you because He loves you. In fact, He loves you so much that He gave His Son's life to win you forgiveness and eternal life. You are very special to God.

Marlene Bagnull

Never Alone

God, You know I'm new at this—
    praying, I mean.
It's all so brand-new, so special.
I know You forgive my sins for Jesus' sake,
    that You sent Him to earth as my Savior,
        but the things I'm learning
          about You now
    are like opening a treasure chest.
You know what I mean, God—
    real treasures, not just stuff.
I'm discovering how much You love me,
    how real You are,
        and how I can trust You
    to help me with my problems.
I'm finding out how exciting it is
    to follow You.
And I'm learning so much about prayer.
Pastor showed me a Bible verse
    that says You want me to talk to You
        about everything.
You really care about what matters to me,
    and I never need to feel alone
        because You are watching over me.
Thank You, God, for inviting me to talk to You.
Help me use this prayer diary
    to write down some of my prayers
        so I'll remember them
          and see Your answers.

Let Him have all your worries and cares, for He is always thinking about you and watching everything that concerns you.
1 Peter 5:7

God, I need to talk to You about _____
_____
_____
_____

Thank You, God, for _____
_____
_____
_____

Help me to _____
_____
_____
_____

In Jesus' name. Amen.

I Resolve

God, You know how every New Year's
     I make a long list of resolutions.
I don't have to tell You
     how I always break them.
But this year it's going to be different.
I'm really going to change some things.
I'm not going to pick fights
     with my brother and sister.
I'm not going to talk back
     to Mom and Dad.
I'm going to study harder,
     and I'm going to exercise.
Those are big resolutions.
Living up to them won't be easy.
If I told anyone else about them,
     they wouldn't believe I could keep them.
And they're right.
I can't!
But You've been showing me, God,
     how I can depend on You.
Nothing is impossible
     with Your help.

Commit everything
you do to the Lord.
Trust Him
to help you do it
and He will.
Psalm 37:5

Thank You, God, for helping me to _____
_____

Please show me how to change _____
_____

Jesus, forgive me for _____
_____

Thank You, God, for _____
_____
_____

In Jesus' name. Amen.

I'm Tired of Being Treated Like a Baby

God, when are my parents going to stop
    treating me like I'm a baby?
My friends can do what they want after school,
    but I have to call and get permission first.
Mom wants to know where I'm at,
    who I'm with,
        and when I'm going to be home.
And if she doesn't like my answers,
    she doesn't have any problem saying no.
It's really embarrassing
    to tell my friends that
        my mother won't let me
          do something.
I don't understand why she has to be so strict.
Doesn't she trust me?
Doesn't she believe I'm able
    to make intelligent decisions?
Today, I was complaining to my friend Lisa.
She gave me a funny look and said I was lucky.
"Lucky!" I screeched.
    "How would you like it
        if your mother wouldn't let you
          do anything?"
"At least I'd know she cares," Lisa said softly.
I can't get what Lisa said out of my mind.
Maybe having all sorts of freedom
    isn't so great after all.
God, I get so confused.
I don't want to be treated like a baby,
    but I don't want to be like Lisa either.
Help me show my parents that I am ready
    for more freedom and responsibility.

"So don't be anxious about tomorrow. God will take care of your tomorrow too. Live one day at a time."
Matthew 6:34

10

God, I need to tell You about _____
_____
_____
_____

God, I want to thank You for _____
_____
_____
_____

God, I need Your help with _____
_____
_____
_____

In Jesus' name. Amen.

I Want to Tell Others, But ...

God, I'm sorry.
I wanted to stand up for what I believe,
        but I guess I also didn't want
                to risk having the kids
                        laugh at me.
I knew what they were doing was wrong.
Why didn't I say so?
Why didn't I tell them I'm a Christian,
        that I don't want to do those things?
I have to admit it, Lord.
I was scared—
        scared I'd be put down for being different.
I wanted to be part of the crowd—
        to be accepted, included.
But suddenly that doesn't mean much
        when I think of how I've disappointed You.
God, please show me what to do
        to make things right.
Give me the courage to let my light shine.
And in the future, God,
        please help me to be
                a real witness for You.

I don't mean to say I am
perfect. I haven't learned
all I should even yet, but I
keep working toward that
day when I will finally be
all that Christ saved me for
and wants me to be.
Philippians 3:12

God, I need to tell You about

_____

_____

_____

God, please forgive me for

_____

_____

_____

God, I need Your help with

_____

_____

_____

In my Savior's name. Amen.

When Are They Going to Grow?

I can't help but notice, God.
Besides, how can I ignore
        the giggles and whispers?
Almost every girl in my class
        is getting them—
                breasts, I mean.
O God, when are mine going to grow?
Why do I have to be different?
I don't want to be flat-chested.
Maybe I should do those exercises
        I've seen on TV.
But I hate to exercise,
        and what would I say
                if my brother caught me?
He already thinks I'm strange.
I know that You say in the Bible that
        "There is a right time for everything."*
God, please let that right time be soon.

But if we must keep trusting God for something
that hasn't happened yet,
it teaches us to wait
patiently and confidently.
Romans 8:25

*See Ecclesiastes 3:1

14

God, I know You have a right time for

_____

_____

_____

Please help me to be patient as I wait for

_____

_____

_____

_____

God, I praise You because

_____

_____

_____

In Jesus' name. Amen.

No One Listens to Me!

It happened again at dinner tonight.
I was saying something
      when my sister interrupted.
"Mom, I was talking first," I complained.
But Mom shushed me.
"This is important," she said.
God, doesn't she know how she made me feel?
Why is nothing that I say
      ever important to anyone around here?
No one is interested in what I do,
      much less in what I think or feel.
I used to try talking to Mom first thing
      when she got home from work.
But usually she had phone calls to return,
      or she was busy with something else,
          and she didn't have time to listen.
And when she did have time,
      she didn't hear me.
Like the thing about my room.
My sister has no business
      poking around my room.
But Mom always sticks up for her.
She never listens to my side of the story.
Sometimes I think it's pointless
      to expect *anyone* to listen to me.
Maybe if I stopped talking they'd begin to wonder.
Maybe they'd even ask me what was wrong.
Fat chance!
They probably would be glad to have me shut up.
God, thank You for always listening,
      even when I complain.
Please help my family listen to me,
      I need them.

I love the Lord because He hears my prayers and answers them. Because He bends down and listens, I will pray as long as I breathe!
Psalm 116:1–2

God, I need to tell You about _____

_____

_____

_____

God, please help me with _____

_____

_____

_____

God, thank You for _____

_____

_____

_____

In my Savior's name. Amen.

My Church Family

Dear God, thank You so much for Sunday.
It's the best day of the week.
I love to listen to Your Word each week.
You have promised to make my faith stronger
    as I listen.
I can remember when I first started
    going to our new church.
I felt lonely and kind of frightened.
I didn't know anyone.
I wondered if I would fit in.
I was anxious to scoot out the door,
    but the pastor stopped me.
"I'm so glad you came," he said.
And the next week, my Sunday school teacher
    also made me feel welcome.
She introduced me to the other kids.
One girl offered to share her Bible
    and even sat with me in church.
Thank You for all the friends I've made
    and for the sharing times in youth group.
It helps to know that other kids
    have some of the same problems I do.
I'm glad we can find answers together in the Bible
    and that we can pray for one another.
Sunday really is a great day.
Thank You, God, for my church family.

Just as there are many parts to our bodies, so it is with Christ's body. We are all parts of it, and it takes every one of us to make it complete, for we each have different work to do. So we belong to each other, and each needs all the others.

Romans 12:4–5

God, I enjoy worshiping You because

_____

_____

Thank You, God, for

_____

_____

_____

_____

Help me to serve my church body by

_____

_____

_____

In Jesus' name. Amen.

In the Beginning

We're studying evolution in science.
My parents are upset about it, God.
They don't think it should be taught
        unless the biblical account of creation
            is taught also.
I've tried to tell them it's okay—
        that I believe what the Bible says.
Nothing else makes much sense to me.
Something as awesome as the universe
        couldn't just happen.
I know You were there from the very beginning,
        and I believe the Bible when it says that
            it's Your power
        "that holds everything together."*
I started thinking about this yesterday
        after Ellen got angry with me
        and said she wasn't going to be my friend.
I was so upset and worried.
Ellen is one of my best friends.
I care about her.
I was trying to figure out
        why she was angry with me.
Suddenly, I thought of how powerful You are—
        how You made the world and preserve it;
        how Jesus defeated sin, death, and the devil
            through His death and resurrection;
        how the Holy Spirit works faith in my heart.
I could hear You say,
        "Is there anything too hard for Me?"
God, I know You know
        all about the problem with Ellen,
        and I also know
        that I can trust You to work things out.

How incredibly great His
power is to help those
who believe Him.
Ephesians 1:19

*See Colossians 1:17

God, I see Your power when _____

_____

_____

I praise You, Lord, for _____

_____

_____

Please help me, God, with _____

_____

_____

In Jesus' name. Amen.

Real Love

I hate Valentine's Day!
I hate all the phony things people say
         on those dumb valentines.
Who needs them?
O God, I do!
It hurt so bad to get so few.
The rest of the year I can pretend
         that I'm popular.
But on Valentine's Day
         the whole class can see
                  that I'm not popular.
I wanted to go home
         and never come back to school.
O God, why don't I have more friends?
I know I have Lisa down the street,
         but sometimes I'm afraid that
                  I'm going to lose her friendship.
If only I could get one valentine
         from someone who really cares about me.
What's that, God?
                  I have?
         It's from Your Son?
                  And it's in the shape of a cross?
I'm sorry. I forgot.
Even though sin kept us from loving Him,
         Jesus chose to love us anyway.
He came to earth to be our Savior.
And because He loves me, I can love Him
         and show love to others.
Thank You, Jesus.
Help me always to remember
         the special valentine You've given me.

We know what real love is
from Christ's example
in dying for us.
1 John 3:16

Thank You, Jesus, for being my
_____

_____

_____

_____

I know You love me, God, because
_____

_____

_____

_____

Help me show love to
_____

_____

_____

_____

In my Savior's name. Amen.

Members Only

Dear God, how could she?
Lisa is supposed to be my friend.
How could she start a club
    and not include me as a member?
You know how I always
    go down to her house after dinner.
Well, tonight a bunch of girls from school
    were sitting on her front steps.
"What is she doing here?"
    I heard one of them whisper.
Lisa got red in the face
    and said something about a new club
    and a "members only" meeting.
"What?" I stammered.
O God, how could she be so mean?
I never did anything to her.
And why didn't Lisa stick up for me?
Before they could see my tears,
    I turned and ran home.
God, I never want to see
    any of those girls again—
        especially Lisa.
But they're in my class!
    What am I going to do?
        How am I going to face them?
What's the matter with me, God?
Why can't I belong?

How they scoff and mock me ... . How they talk about me ... . But I keep right on praying to You, Lord. For now is the time—You are bending down to hear! You are ready with a plentiful supply of love and kindness.
Psalm 69:10–11, 13

24

God, I felt I didn't belong when

_____

_____

_____

_____

Lord, be with me as I

_____

_____

_____

Thank You, God, for

_____

_____

In Jesus' name I pray. Amen.

The New Girl

God, why do kids have to be so mean?
They aren't giving the new girl a chance.
They started making fun of her
      the first day she came to school.
Yesterday she was crying
      when we passed in the hallway.
Later, I heard how she somehow missed the table
      when she set down her lunch tray—
         how her orange went rolling,
      and her milk splattered everywhere.
Would I have laughed too,
      if I had been there,
         or would I have had the courage
      to stand up for her?
I think I know what I would have done, God,
      and it doesn't make me feel good,
         especially when I remember
      what I learned in Sunday school
         about Esther.
She could have kept silent.
It would have been a lot easier and safer.
Instead she risked her life
      to save her people.
God, I want to be like Esther.
I want to think about others—
      not just myself.
I want to have the courage to do Your will,
      even if it means the kids
         will make fun of me too.
Please, God, help me to be wise and brave
      like beautiful Queen Esther.
Show me how I can help the new girl.
Show me what You want me to do.

You should defend those who cannot help themselves. Yes, speak up for the poor and needy and see that they get justice.
Proverbs 31:8–9

To learn more about Esther, read the Old Testament book named for her.

God, show me how to help

_____

_____

_____

Forgive me for not doing Your will, especially when

_____

_____

_____

Thank You, God, for

_____

_____

_____

In my Savior's name I pray. Amen.

Sticks and Stones

"Sticks and stones may break your bones,
        but names will never hurt you."
God, that's what my dad says.
I try to remember it.
        I try to say that to myself
                when the kids tease me.
But it *does* hurt.
It hurts so bad.
I can't pretend I don't hear
        or just laugh it off.
Every day before recess,
        I get a knot in my stomach.
It's no fun to go outside—
        to be left out and called names.
God, help me to remember,
        like my pastor taught in church,
                the names You call me:
        "Friend." "Dear one." "Beloved child."
Help me to hear Your words
        instead of the mean things the kids say.

See how very much our
heavenly Father loves us,
for He allows us to be
called His children—think
of it—and we really *are!*
1 John 3:1

God, I hurt when

_____

_____

_____

Lord, remind me of

_____

_____

_____

Thank You, God, for

_____

_____

_____

In my Best Friend's name. Amen.

My Room

God, I don't understand
      why Mom is always
            on me about my room.
It's my room!
I don't mind the way it looks.
If she doesn't like it,
      why doesn't she close the door?
Doesn't she know that
      I'm no different than other kids?
Their rooms are messy too.
I'm normal!
I'd rather talk on the phone,
      watch television,
         play outside,
            or even read a book
      than clean my room.
But it does make Mom unhappy,
      and I know You want me to
      "honor" my parents.
I guess taking care of my room
      is part of that.
God, help me to be less sloppy,
      and help Mom to expect a little less.

Children, obey your parents; this is the right thing to do because God has placed them in authority over you.
Ephesians 6:1

God, sometimes my parents make me

_____

_____

_____

Lord, please help me and my parents

_____

_____

_____

Thank You, God, for

_____

_____

_____

_____

In Jesus' name. Amen.

A Lenten Commitment

God, today some kids
came to school with ashes
on their foreheads.
We don't do that at our church,
but on Sunday, Pastor did ask us
to think about something "significant"
that we could do to remember You
during Lent.
I know some people give up things for Lent.
I guess that could be a good way to remind
ourselves of how Jesus gave His life
to win us forgiveness for our sins.
I've thought of things I could give up—
candy, gum, snacks, TV shows …
It's not that I don't want to give them up,
but I wonder if it might mean more
to *do* something
instead of to *give up* something.
What I mean is,
what if I made a commitment
to read my Bible every day
during Lent?
I think that would be a lot more important.
Maybe I could read one of the gospels
and the book of Acts.
I've never read a gospel from beginning to end,
and I would like to know the whole story
of how the church got started.
I'd have to read a little more than a chapter a day.
God, I'm glad it's the first day of Lent.
I'm glad I can use this time
to learn more about You
and Your plan of salvation through Jesus.

Remember what Christ
taught and let His words
enrich your lives and
make you wise.
Colossians 3:16

God, during Lent, I remember _____

_____

_____

Please forgive me for Jesus' sake for _____

_____

_____

Help me to make a commitment during Lent to _____

_____

_____

In my Savior's name. Amen.

Tryouts

O God, Mom says I should try out
        for the school choir.
She knows how much I love to sing.
She's trying to encourage me,
        but I'd rather forget the whole thing.
I remember when I tried out last year—
        and didn't make it.
I felt like I made a total fool of myself.
My voice cracked on the low notes
        and squeaked on the high ones.
I wanted to run when I heard the giggles.
Mom said it was stage fright—
        that I would get over it.
But what if I'm not over it yet?
I don't want to be laughed at again.
God, You know I've been practicing.
You know that I want to use my talent
        to praise You.
Help me trust You to help me
        not to be so frightened.

Fear not, for I am with
you. Do not be dismayed.
I am your God. I will
strengthen you;
I will help you.
Isaiah 41:10

Thank You, God, for the ability You gave me to

_____

_____

_____

Show me ways to use my talents for You, like

_____

_____

_____

Give me strength, Lord, to

_____

_____

_____

In Jesus' name. Amen.

I Hate Boys!

God, how come You had to make boys—
    at least boys like John and Brian?
I hate them!
I'm sorry, God.
I know I'm not supposed to hate anybody,
    but can't they be the exception?
My sister says they act the way they do
    because they like me.
Well, I sure think
    they have a dumb way of showing it.
Brian calls me names
    and draws pictures of me.
John always has something smart to say.
As far as I'm concerned
    boys are nothing but pests.
I can live without them—
    especially without John and Brian.
But there are these two older guys
    who are really cute.
My heart pounds in a funny way
    every time I see them.
Yesterday, one of them smiled at me.
Do You think he likes me—
    I mean *really* likes me?
I'm so confused, God.
How can I hate boys
    and like them at the same time?
Why does it matter so much
    how they feel about me?
Do boys wonder about the same things?

For how well He under-
stands us and knows what
is best for us at all times.
Ephesians 1:8

God, I need to talk to You about

_____

_____

Sometimes I get so upset about

_____

_____

I feel happy when

_____

_____

Thank You, God, for

_____

_____

In Jesus' name. Amen.

Best Friends

O God, do You know how good I feel
　　　now that I'm friends with Lisa again?
The last few days have been awful.
I didn't mean the things I said to Lisa.
I guess I was just jealous
　　　because she got a better grade
　　　　　on her social studies report.
I was afraid she'd never forgive me.
I could hardly believe it
　　　when she invited me to spend the night.
We had so much fun!
We hardly slept at all.
I bet her mom and dad didn't either.
But we had more than just a fun time.
I told her I was sorry.
Lisa said she was sorry too
　　　and that she was as miserable as I was.
She couldn't stand the thought
　　　of losing her "best friend."
God, I didn't know she felt that way about me.
I've felt the same way about her,
　　　but I've never had the nerve to tell her.
Last night we talked about really important stuff,
　　　things we've never shared before.
We talked about You too, God.
It was as if You were right in the room with us.
It feels so good to know I have a friend,
　　　a *best* friend,
　　　　　I can trust and confide in.
Thank You, God,
　　　for giving me a friend like Lisa.
Help us always to be best friends.

A friend loves at all times.
Proverbs 17:17 NIV

God, thank You for my friends, including

_____

_____

_____

I have so much fun when my friends and I

_____

_____

_____

I know You are with us because

_____

_____

Keep us close to one another and to You.

In Jesus' name. Amen.

_____

God, Did You Forget Me?

God, I hope You won't get angry
        when I ask this,
                but did You forget me
        when You were handing out
                brains and talents?
Mom says I'm average,
        but I know what she's really thinking.
I hear her bragging about my sister and brother,
        but she never brags about me.
I've never gotten an *A* in any subject.
I probably never will.
My greatest talent is
        making other people laugh—
                at me.
God, if only there was *one* thing
        I could do really well.
Isn't there some hidden talent,
        some gift,
                some *something* that I can do?
I tried skating,
        but I sprained my ankle.
Gymnastics is a joke.
Can You imagine coordinated me
        on a balance beam?
I've tried some group sports,
        but I can't seem to get the hang
                of all the rules.
I thought about taking music lessons,
        but Mom says we can't afford them.
Seriously, God,
        did You forget about me?

I made you, and I will not
forget to help you.
Isaiah 44:21

God, thank You for the ability to

_____

_____

_____

Please help me, Lord, not to be jealous of

_____

_____

_____

Remind me, God, that You have not forgotten me,
especially when

_____

_____

In Jesus' name. Amen.

You Love Me That Much!

Pastor gave me a lot to think about today.
His sermon said so much about
      how much Jesus loves us—
          how much He loves me!
He gave us an outline
      of the events of Holy Week.
I know all about Palm Sunday and Easter,
      and I go to the Maundy Thursday
      and Good Friday services with my parents,
But I haven't stopped to think much
      about the details of what happened.
Like the crucifixion.
I don't like to think about it,
        but Pastor said it's important
      to remember how Jesus suffered and died.
But he also said—
      and I can't get it out of my mind—
      that Jesus didn't have to die.
"He could have come down from the cross,"
      Pastor said,
      "but He chose to hang there
        because He loves us that much."
I remembered last week
      when I was in the dentist's chair.
I sure wouldn't have stayed there
      if I didn't have to,
        and it hardly hurt.
Thank You, Jesus,
      for loving me enough to hang on the cross.
And thank You even more for rising from the dead.
Because of Your resurrection,
      I will live with You in heaven forever.

"As the Father has loved Me, so have I loved you. ... Greater love has no one than this, that he lay down his life for his friends."
John 15:9, 13 NIV

God, I don't understand how You can love me, especially when _____

_____

_____

Forgive me for _____

_____

_____

Thank You for sending Jesus to be my Savior and for _____

_____

_____

_____ In my Savior's name. Amen.

Report Card Blues

Dear God, I wish I could lose my report card,
    but what good would that do?
My parents are going to be so angry.
They won't believe that I really tried.
I don't know why
    I got such an awful grade in science.
I pay attention in class,
    but I just don't understand
        the stuff we're studying.
Everyone else seems to get it, though.
Why not me?
And I have been taking my time
    to try to write neatly.
The girl behind me got an A in handwriting.
Why did I only get a C?
    My writing looks like hers.
I know my parents will say
    I have to try harder.
But what happens when my best
    isn't good enough?
God, please make them believe
    that I really did try.

Don't worry about any-
thing; instead, pray about
everything; tell God your
needs and don't forget to
thank Him for His answers.
Philippians 4:6

44

God, I'm worried about

_____

_____

_____

_____

Point me to people who can help me with

_____

_____

_____

_____

Thank You, God, for

_____

_____

_____

In Jesus' name. Amen.

_____

I Trusted Her!

She promised she wouldn't tell anyone, God.
I trusted her!
I feel like such a fool.
Now the whole class knows that I like Eric,
        and he's telling everyone
                he can't stand me!
I wish we could move
        or that I had the courage to run away.
But where could I go?
What can I do?
How long will it take the kids to forget?
How long will it take *me* to forget
        that my best friend can't be trusted?
God, I'm so glad that I can trust You.
You've promised never to let me down.
Thank You, God.

For God has said,
"I will never, *never* fail
you nor forsake you."
Hebrews 13:5

God, I feel betrayed when

_____

_____

_____

Forgive me for betraying You when

_____

_____

_____

Help me to show love to others when

_____

_____

_____

In my Savior's name. Amen.

Timid and Trembling

God, those are the last words
   I would ever use
      to describe the apostle Paul.
We've been studying about him in Sunday school.
Paul probably told more people about You
   than anyone else.
He had the courage to face beatings
   and shipwrecks—even imprisonment—
      to share the Good News of Jesus.
In the end he was beheaded
   because he refused to deny
      his faith in You.
Yet in the letter Paul wrote to the Corinthians,
   he said,
      "I came to you in weakness—
         timid and trembling."*
I don't understand how he could act so brave
   yet be so frightened inside.
Pastor said it takes courage
   to admit you're afraid.
He said that You don't expect us
   never to feel fearful.
Pastor said he gets frightened
      about lots of things—
   even about preaching on Sundays.
I was shocked.
He never seems frightened or nervous.
Pastor said something else that
   I hope I'll always remember.
He said fear can be something very positive
   if it causes us to rely on You.

Stand steady, and don't
be afraid of suffering for
the Lord. Bring others to
Christ. Leave nothing
undone that you
ought to do.
2 Timothy 4:5

*See 1 Corinthians 2:3

God, thank You for the Bible, which shows me

_____

_____

_____

When I'm afraid, remind me of Your promises,
including

_____

_____

Help me to tell others about Jesus, my Savior,
especially

_____

_____

In Jesus' name. Amen.
_____

Stand Up Straight!

Dear God, I'm so tired
      of Mom lecturing me and telling me to
          "Stand up straight!"
She always picks a time
      when one of my friends is around.
Doesn't she know how she embarrasses me?
Doesn't she understand
      that I slouch because I'm a head taller
          than anyone else in my class?
I hate being different!
I hate standing out in a crowd, literally!
Remember the special assembly last week
      when my class sang those songs?
I saw some kids pointing and laughing.
I knew it was at me.
My teacher put me in the middle of the back row
      with all the boys.
I stuck out—up—
      like a sore thumb.
Mom says that someday I'll stop growing
      and the others will catch up.
Until then, God,
      please help me not to be so self-conscious.
Help me to stand tall and proud
      because You made me.

He will keep in perfect peace all those who trust in Him, whose thoughts turn often to the Lord! Trust in the Lord God always, for in the Lord Jehovah is your everlasting strength.
Isaiah 26:3–4

God, I need to talk to You about _____

_____

_____

_____

Forgive me for Jesus' sake when I _____

_____

_____

Keep me safe from _____

_____

_____

In Jesus' name. Amen.

The Spirit and Me

O God, there's so much I don't understand
    when I read the Bible.
I don't understand how frightened fishermen
    could be changed on the day of Pentecost.
I don't understand how the Holy Spirit
    can fill and change me too,
        but I know He's at work in my life.
I like the things the Bible says
    about the Holy Spirit being my Helper,
        Comforter,
            Teacher.
It also says He will help me
    tell others about You.
I don't understand how He will turn
    my weak knees, trembling voice, and
        tiny actions
    into a powerful witness.
I guess that doesn't matter
    because You will make it happen, not me.
I need all the power You can give me
    to live as a Christian.
I need the Holy Spirit
    to help me avoid doing wrong things,
        to comfort me when I feel lonely
          and frightened,
        to teach me what I need to learn,
        to help me share the Good News
          with others.
Thank You for Your promise
    that when I ask I will receive.
Thank You, God, for giving me Your Holy Spirit.

"But you will receive power when the Holy Spirit comes on you; and you will be My witnesses in Jerusalem, and in all Judea and Samaria, and to the ends of the earth."
Acts 1:8 NIV

God, send Your Holy Spirit to _____

_____

_____

_____

Thank You, God, for _____

_____

_____

_____

Be with me, God, as I _____

_____

_____

_____

In my Savior's name I pray. Amen.

Temper Tantrums

Dear God, my temper has always gotten me
    in trouble.
When I was little, I would lie on the floor,
    kick my feet, and scream
        when I didn't get my way.
When Mom ignored me,
        I would get even angrier—
           and louder.
I don't throw temper tantrums anymore,
    but there are times I'd like to.
Like today.
I got really angry at one of my teachers.
As soon as I got to my locker,
        I started throwing stuff around.
Okay, I know it was childish,
        but I had to blow off steam somehow.
One of my friends asked what was wrong.
I was telling her all about what happened
        when who should I see behind me
           but the teacher.
He must have heard everything!
O God, I'm so embarrassed.
I'm supposed to be a Christian,
        yet I let my temper get the best of me
           again.
Please forgive me, Lord, for losing my temper.
Help me learn to respond with love,
        like Jesus did,
      instead of with hateful words.
Remind me to think before I speak or act.
I know You can help me work on this, God.

But when the Holy Spirit controls our lives He will produce this kind of fruit in us: love, joy, peace, patience, kindness, goodness, faithfulness, gentleness and self-control.
Galatians 5:22–23

God, I need Your help to deal with

_____

_____

_____

_____

Help me obey Your command to love others,
especially

_____

_____

Forgive me for Jesus' sake when

_____

_____

In my Savior's name. Amen.

Excuses

O God, I tried to tell Mr. Grant that
       it wasn't my fault,
               but he didn't believe me.
"It's your responsibility
       to turn your work in on time," he insisted.
"But I had to go to the dentist after school,
       and there wasn't time in the evening."
"You've known for a month
       when this report was due," Mr. Grant said.
"But I got started late because the library
       didn't have all the books I needed."
I had some more excuses ready,
       but I knew that they wouldn't help.
Why did I wait until the last minute?
Now Mr. Grant is going to bring my grade down
       one letter for each day I'm late.
I told Mom.
I thought maybe she'd write a note or something.
But Mom said hopefully this would teach me
       to stop making excuses.
Doesn't she care whether I pass or fail?
My brother overheard me grumbling to Lisa.
"I had to learn the hard way too," he said.
"Just like you, I was good at making excuses
       for things I should have done but didn't.
When I missed the district track meet
       because I forgot to get
       the permission slip signed,
               I decided it was time to change."
God, I know You were talking to me through
       my brother.
Show me how to break my bad habit.
       I know that You will help me do Your will.

And you will know the
truth, and the truth will
set you free.
John 8:32

God, thank You for the lesson You taught me about

God, help me to follow You, even when

forgive me when I

In Jesus' name. Amen.

Who Has More Fun?

I couldn't believe it, God.
Susan came to school today with blonde hair!
She had talked about dyeing her hair,
      but I never thought she'd do it—
          or that her mother would let her.
I know mine wouldn't.
But Susan said it's her hair,
      and she wanted to find out
          if blondes really do have more fun.
I didn't tell her what I thought.
Oh, her hair looks okay,
      but I doubt she'll have more "fun."
You see, Susan's kind of like me, God.
Neither one of us is beautiful.
      Neither one of us has breasts yet.
Why would the color of her hair
      make much difference?
I know who has more fun.
It's the girls who are good-looking.
They have more friends.
They get invited to everything.
They *do* have more fun!
But Mom says there are more important things
      than being beautiful and having fun.
I wonder if she said that
      when she was a teenager?
I don't know why You made me the way You did,
      but help me to make the most
         of what I've got
      and to find those "more important things"
         Mom keeps talking about.

Charm can be deceptive
and beauty doesn't last,
but a woman who fears
and reverences God shall
be greatly praised.
Proverbs 31:30

God, thank You for the wonderful parts of me, like

_____

_____

_____

Forgive me when I complain about

_____

_____

_____

Help me see the positives in my life, including

_____

_____

_____

In Jesus' name. Amen.

Nothing Is Impossible

Do You remember how I felt, God,
      when Mom and Dad said we were moving?
I cried myself to sleep that night
      thinking about how hard it would be
         to say good-bye to my friends—
And how hard it would be to make new ones.
I begged You to make Mom and Dad change
      their minds.
You didn't and they didn't,
      and more quickly than I expected
       our things were loaded into a moving van.
I was convinced it was the worst day of my life.
Lisa came to say good-bye.
She promised to write.
I nodded my head that I would too.
I was afraid I'd start crying if I tried to talk.
It was hard
      getting used to our new house.
It didn't feel like home.
I didn't see any girls my age in the neighborhood
      or in the church we visited.
Going to school was the hardest.
I thought I'd never find my classes.
I don't think I ever prayed as much
      as I did those first few weeks.
But something special began to happen.
I discovered that You really were with me.
That must have been what happened to Abraham
      when You told him to leave home.
He didn't even know where he was going!
But Abraham trusted You.
He knew that You were always with him.
Thank You, God, for teaching me the same thing.

"*Anything* is possible if you have faith."
Mark 9:23

To learn more about Abraham, read Genesis 12:1–9 and Genesis 15:1–6.

God, I know You will help me with

Thank You, Lord, for

Keep me safe as I

In Jesus' name. Amen.

My Birthday

Today is my birthday, God.
I wish I could have more than one a year.
Mom just laughs
            and says I won't feel that way
                        when I get older.
I can hardly wait until the party this afternoon.
Four of my friends from school are coming.
We're going to the movies.
Afterward we'll come back here
            for cake and ice cream
                        and to open my gifts.
I've been counting the days for weeks
            and worrying some too, God.
You see my party is the same day as Kathy's,
            and even the movies can't top
                        the neat parties she always has.
Everybody wants to go to her parties.
I was afraid no one
            would want to come to mine.
I begged Mom to let me hand out 10 invitations.
"I can't afford to take all those kids
            to the movies,"
                        she said.
I didn't know how to explain to her
            what I just told You.
I didn't want to admit out loud that I was afraid
            no one would come.
Finally, Mom agreed I could invite six people.
Please, God, don't let anything spoil
            this special day.

Lord, when doubts fill my
mind, when my heart is in
turmoil, quiet me
and give me renewed
hope and cheer.
Psalm 94:19

God, on my birthday, I especially ask for

_____

_____

_____

_____

Thank You, Father, for the wonderful things that
happened this year, including

_____

_____

Protect me during this next year as I

_____

_____

In my Savior's name I pray. Amen.

But I'm Not Them!

Dear God, why do my parents compare me
                to my brother and sister?
I'm not them!
Just because my sister is a brain,
                it's not fair to expect me to be;
                                but Mom and Dad do.
                And so do the teachers
                        who have had my sister before me.
I still remember how my face turned red
                the first day Mrs. Hunter took attendance.
"Oh, yes," she said when she got to my name.
                "I had your sister, didn't I?
                She was such a good student."
I heard some of the kids start to giggle.
Even they know there's no comparison
                between me and my sister.
And just because both my sister and brother
                are good in sports,
                                does that mean I have to be?
Mom and Dad are always urging me
                to go out for stuff.
But I'm not the athletic type!
Why can't Mom and Dad understand that?
Why do they have to compare me to others?
O God, I feel like
                they're so disappointed in me—
                                like they wish they hadn't had me.
I feel like some kind of mistake.
Can't anyone love me just the way I am?

May you be able to feel and understand, as all God's children should, how long, how wide, how deep, and how high His love really is; and to experience this love for yourselves, though it is so great that you will never see the end of it or fully know or understand it.
Ephesians 3:18–19

God, I know You love me because

_____

_____

_____

Help my parents understand it hurts me when

_____

_____

_____

Show me the many ways You have made me
unique, like

_____

_____

_____

In Jesus' name. Amen.

The Candy Sale

God, I've had it!
I carried that carton of candy
     all over the neighborhood.*
"We already bought some from someone else,"
     Mrs. Brown said.
"My granddaughter is selling wrapping paper,"
     the man on the corner said.
"I don't want any,"
     others said with a frown.
I sold only four boxes in two whole hours!
What am I going to do?
I'm supposed to sell 24 boxes,
     and a lot of kids will sell even more.
How come they can sell this stuff and I can't?
I even prayed before I went to each door.
Why didn't You help me?
You said I can do all things through You.
Doesn't that include selling candy?
I guess I just have to keep trying.
Dad says that if things come too easy,
     I won't appreciate them.
I guess I just have to keep trusting You,
     even when I wonder if You're listening.

We can rejoice, too, when we run into problems and trials for we know that they are good for us—they help us learn to be patient. And patience develops strength of character in us and helps us trust God more each time we use it.
Romans 5:3–4

*Whenever you're selling anything, be sure to go only to people you know. It's also best not to go alone.

God, I need Your help to

_____

_____

_____

Show me the many ways You're at work in my
life, like

_____

_____

_____

Forgive me for Jesus' sake when

_____

_____

In my Savior's name. Amen.

Facing School

Just one more week, God,
     until school starts.
One minute I can hardly wait,
     and the next minute I'm dreading it.
I'm a mixture of confused feelings.
I wish I had kept in touch with my school friends
     during the summer.
I intended to,
     and they said they would call me,
        but with vacations
           and everything ...
I can't believe summer has gone so fast.
In some ways I'm ready for it to be over,
     but in other ways I'm not.
I really wasn't as bored
     as I complained to Mom,
        but I did get lonely sometimes.
I guess that's what scares me, God.
What if I'm just as lonely
     when I get back to school?
What if everyone has made new friends
     and no one wants to be friends with me?
What if I don't know anyone in my classes?
What if all my teachers are tough?
I'm sorry, God.
I know I'm letting fear take the place of faith.
Thank You
     that I don't have to go to school alone.
I know You'll go with me,
     and I know that with Your help,
        I am going to have a great year.

But when I am afraid, I will put my confidence in You. Yes, I will trust the promises of God.
Psalm 56:3

God, I like school because
_____
_____
_____

Sometimes I'm afraid of school because
_____
_____
_____

Remind me, Lord, that You're with me and will
help me when
_____
_____
_____

In Jesus' name. Amen.

Who Me, God?

God, I think Moses is my favorite person
in the whole Bible—
not because of all the brave
and important things he did,
but because he didn't think
he could do any of them.
He had as many excuses, doubts, and fears
as I often have.
He told You he wasn't the person for the job.
How would he know what to say to people?
Who would believe him or listen to him?
He reminded You how he wasn't a good speaker.
I can imagine that Moses wanted to run
as far away as he could
from what You were asking him
to do.
I'm glad You told us all about Moses.
It helps to know
that I'm not the only one who says,
"Who me, God?"
If You could use Moses,
then I know You can use me too.
I'm still frightened about telling other kids
about You
and trying to live as You want me to.
But if You'll be with me as You were with Moses,
I know You will help me do my best.

"Now go ahead and do as
I tell you, for I will help
you to speak well, and I
will tell you what to say."
Exodus 4:12

To learn more
about Moses, read
Exodus 3:1–4:31

God, thank You for the Bible. In it I learn so much about You as I read about

_____

Forgive me when I try to run away from my responsibilities. Help me work for You as I

_____

Point me to the best ways to use my talents for You, including

_____

In Jesus' name. Amen.

Metal Mouth

God, why couldn't You have made me
with straight, beautiful teeth?
I hate braces!
And I hate it when Mom says,
"Someday you'll be glad you wore them."
What do I care about "someday"
when they're making my life
miserable today?
If Brian calls me "Metal Mouth" one more time,
I'm going to sock him.
Maybe I can knock his teeth out of place
so he'll need to wear braces too.
I'm sorry, God.
I know I shouldn't even think such a thing.
But Brian makes me so angry!
I wish he would leave me alone,
and I wish I'd get these braces off—now,
not in a year or two.
That seems like forever.
Then, I think about the time Your Son
hung on the cross.
That must have seemed like forever to Him.
But Jesus didn't complain about the pain
or get angry at the people
who made fun of Him.
When I think about what He went through,
it makes my problem with braces
seem very small.
Jesus, please help me remember this
the next time Brian
calls me "Metal Mouth."
Help me to be more like You.

Keep your eyes on Jesus,
our leader and instructor.
He was willing to die a
shameful death on the
cross because of the joy
He knew would be His
afterwards.
Hebrews 12:2

God, I'm having trouble with _____

_____

_____

_____

Please, Lord, help me turn the other cheek when ___

_____

_____

_____

Thank You, God, for _____

_____

_____

_____

In my Savior's name. Amen.

They Laughed at Him Too

God, it must have seemed ridiculous,
    even to Noah—building a boat
        on dry land, I mean.
I can almost hear his neighbors laughing.
The Bible says the boat
    was longer than a football field!
They must have thought Noah was a real fool.
Even if there had been water nearby,
    how would he ever get the boat to it?
But Noah did exactly what You said;
        and after the boat was finished,
    he started bringing animals on board.
I can see Noah struggling with an elephant or lion
    and hear his neighbors roaring.
But that didn't stop Noah
    from following Your instructions.
And it's a good thing he did what You said,
    otherwise he and his family would have
        drowned in the Flood.
I can see there are a lot of things
    I need to learn from Noah.
Like learning not to let it bother me
    when kids laugh at me
        for being a Christian.
They can't understand
    why I won't do some of the things they do,
    so they tease me and make fun of me.
It isn't easy to be different.
But when I see some of my old friends
    getting in trouble,
        I'm so glad I follow You.
Keep me close to You forever.

If someone mistreats you because you are a Christian, don't curse him; pray that God will bless him.
Romans 12:14

To learn more about Noah, read Genesis 6:1–9:17

74

God, sometimes I don't understand why You want
me to _____

_____

When others make fun of me for being a Christian,
remind me of _____

_____

Thank You for the gift of faith. I know that
through it, I have _____

_____

In my Savior's name. Amen.

Nightmares

Dear God, I keep having this scary nightmare.
I fall in the street.
A truck is coming.
I can't get up
         or even roll over.
I don't know what happens next.
I wake up right at that moment.
I'm frightened, God,
         and not just by my dream.
I'm afraid of growing up.
I'm afraid of things that may happen to me.
I can't always go running home to Mom and Dad.
But will I know what to do
         when I face problems?
What if I make a serious mistake?
Will I freeze like I do in my dream?
Will I end up just making a mess
         out of my life?
Suddenly, I remember reading in the Bible
         how You've promised to walk beside me.
I don't need to be frightened
         because You are with me.
Thank You, God.

He will never let me stumble, slip or fall. For He is always watching, never sleeping.
Psalm 121:3–4

God, I get scared when _____

_____

_____

Remind me that You are with me as I face

_____

_____

_____

Thank You, God, for _____

_____

_____

In Jesus' name. Amen.

One Little White Lie

It was just one little white lie.
I didn't think it would hurt anything,
      but then I also didn't think
            Ellen would repeat it.
O God, why couldn't she
      keep her mouth shut?
I didn't know what to say
      when someone else asked me
            what I had said to Ellen.
There was nothing I could do
      but tell another lie
            and another and another.
Now I'm in so deep
      I don't see any way out.
Why didn't I tell the truth
      in the first place?
Okay, I know why, and so do You.
It was easier.
It made me look good,
      but now I'm going to look like a fool
            when the truth catches up
                  with me.
I sure got myself into a mess.
I only hope I've learned my lesson.
From now on,
      I'm going to say nothing but the truth.
         Please help me, God.

The Lord's promise is sure.
He speaks no careless
word; all He says is purest
truth, like silver seven
times refined.
Psalm 12:6

God, I have trouble telling the truth when
_____
_____
_____

Forgive me for lying, especially about
_____
_____
_____

Help me tell the truth, even when
_____
_____
_____

In Jesus' name. Amen.

Thank You, God

Mom has the turkey in the oven.
She baked the pies yesterday.
I can imagine our Thanksgiving table.
It will be so full that
        there hardly will be room for our plates.
Every Thanksgiving that I can remember
        has been a day of joy and feasting.
Before we eat,
        we go around the table and tell something
                we're especially thankful for.
I've been thinking of what I would say this year.
I realize I'm not always thankful
        for the ways You have blessed me.
I look at things other kids have
        and wish they were mine.
I'm not satisfied
        with the way You've made me.
I want to be prettier and smarter—
        more talented.
I want to have more friends.
But this year I've gotten to know someone
        who has made me aware
                of how lucky I really am.
Nancy comes to school in a wheelchair.
She can't run and play,
        and she doesn't have a lot of friends.
But Nancy keeps smiling.
She told me that she's a Christian,
        and You know, God, it shows.
This Thanksgiving,
        I'm going to share how I'm thankful
                for the things You've taught me
                        through Nancy.

Say "Thank You" to the
Lord for being so good,
for always being so loving
and kind.
Psalm 107:1

God, thank You for people like _____

_____

_____

Thank You for how they have taught me to _____

_____

_____

_____

Thank You also for _____

_____

_____

_____

In Jesus' name. Amen.

Hiding

Today, I was reading about Jonah.
I don't know why I opened my Bible
to that book,
but I think You do, God.
You know how I've been kind of hiding
from You—
ignoring what I know You want me to do.
I haven't wanted
to tell the kids in the neighborhood
that I'm a Christian.
Once I do, I'll have to take a stand
about some of the things they do
that I know aren't right.
Jonah also wanted You to use somebody else.
He ran in the opposite direction
of the way You wanted him to go.
He got on a ship and hid in the hold.
There was a storm at sea,
and Jonah ended up
in the belly of a great fish.
But You rescued Jonah
and gave him another chance to do
what You wanted him to do.
God, forgive me for not wanting
to do Your will.
Help me not to run away and hide.

Love the Lord and follow
His plan for your lives.
Cling to Him and serve
Him enthusiastically.
Joshua 22:5

To learn more about
Jonah read the Old
Testament book named
for him.

God, sometimes I hide from You because
_____
_____
_____

Forgive me when I avoid You. Show me Your will about
_____
_____
_____

Thank You for rescuing me when
_____
_____
_____

In Jesus' name. Amen.
_____

The Lord Is in His Holy Temple

I was so embarrassed, God.
Pastor saw me and Ellen giggling
     and passing notes in church.
He said something to me after the service
     I don't think I'll ever forget.
He reminded me how the church is Your temple
     and how we come here to worship You.
"Have you stopped to think how God feels
     when you fool around?" he asked.
I'm sorry, God.
I never thought about how I make You feel.
I try to pay attention to the sermon,
     but sometimes it gets boring.
The words of the hymns
     don't always make a lot of sense to me,
          so I don't always bother to sing.
And my mind has a way of wandering
     during my prayers.
It was almost as if Pastor read my thoughts.
"The sermon and hymns and prayers
     are all important," he said.
"But the most important reason
     we come to church is to listen
          to what God has to say to us."
I felt my cheeks get hot.
I haven't been listening, God.
I guess I figured we'd talk later
     when *I* had something to say.
I never thought *You* might want to talk to me.
God, I don't want to hurt Your feelings.
I don't want to miss anything You have to say.
Teach me how to listen
     and how to really worship You.

"But the Lord is in His holy temple; let all the earth be silent before Him."
Habakkuk 2:20

God, I like church because

_____

_____

_____

Forgive me when I ignore You in church as I

_____

_____

_____

Thank You for speaking to me in Your Word about

_____

_____

_____

In Jesus' name. Amen.

And the Walls Came Tumbling Down

What an incredible story, God.
You told Joshua to march the army
    around Jericho for six days.
On the seventh day they were to blow trumpets,
    and You said the walls would crumble.
I wonder if any of the soldiers grumbled?
Forgive me, God,
    but it did seem like a stupid thing to do.
But Joshua and his men obeyed,
    and You kept Your promise.
The walls did come tumbling down.
I've been thinking about this story
    ever since we studied it in Sunday school.
I've been wondering
    what You want me to learn from it.
Suddenly, I thought of the problem
    I've been having with Karen.
She's never said anything nice to me.
I don't know why she doesn't like me—
    why she has to be so mean.
I have tried practicing the Golden Rule—
    treating her like I want her to treat me—
        but it hasn't worked.
I decided I would quit trying to be nice to her.
But just now You've reminded me
    how I'm supposed to love my enemies.
That doesn't make much more sense
    than walking around the walls of Jericho.
But I have this strange feeling of excitement.
I know You will be at work
    and bring about something good.

This plan of Mine is not what you would work out, neither are My thoughts the same as yours! For just as the heavens are higher than the earth, so are My ways higher than yours, and My thoughts than yours.
Isaiah 55:8–9

To learn more about Joshua, read Joshua 1:1–6:27.

God, I'm having trouble understanding _____

_____

_____

_____

Show me how to deal with _____

_____

_____

_____

I know You will work for good in these situations: _____

_____

_____

_____

In my Savior's name. Amen.

A Girl Like Me

Sunday school was really neat today, God.
We talked about Mary.
My teacher said she was just an ordinary girl.
Her parents weren't rich or famous.
She lived in Nazareth—
>   a town that didn't have a good name.
But You chose Mary to become
>   the mother of Jesus, Your Son.
When the angel came to her,
>   Mary was frightened and confused.
I can imagine her pointing to herself
>   and saying, "Who, me?"
But Mary believed the angel's words.
She said she was willing to do
>   whatever You wanted.
I felt my heart racing as my teacher
>   got to the point of the lesson.
She said, "God may be calling any one of you
>   to do something special for Him.
You'll probably think He's made a mistake—
>   that someone else is more qualified—
But God doesn't see you as you see yourself.
>   God knows what you can become."
I hoped my cheeks weren't getting red.
You see, I've never told anyone
>   how I've been thinking about
>   working in a church profession
>   when I grow up.
I figured people would wonder
>   who I thought I was.
But if Mary was just an ordinary girl,
>   then maybe I'm not just dreaming.
Help me to say yes like she did, God.

Mary said, "I am the Lord's servant, and I am willing to do whatever He wants."
Luke 1:38

God, I've been thinking a lot about

_____

_____

_____

I'm not sure what I want to be when I grow up.
Please show me what You think about

_____

_____

_____

God, thank You for letting me serve You as I

_____

_____

In Jesus' name. Amen.

The Greatest Gift

Only three days until Christmas
I wish the time would go faster.
I can't wait to see what Mom and Dad got me.
You know I've been poking around for weeks
        trying to find out where
                they've hidden my gifts.
Yet I really don't want to find them.
I don't want to spoil the surprise.
Besides, they couldn't hide
        what I want more than anything else.
Oh, how I hope they've gotten me a horse!
That would be the greatest gift ever.
At least that was what I thought
        until Pastor's sermon this morning.
It was strange.
I felt like he was speaking right to me.
He talked about how You gave us
        the greatest gift of all.
I'm sorry, God.
I never stopped to think
        what it cost You that first Christmas.
It must have been hard
        to send Your Son to earth,
                especially since You knew
        He would have to die on a cross.
And Pastor said
        even if I were the only person on earth,
                Jesus still would have come
        and died just for me.
I can't imagine You loving me that much,
        but I'm glad You do.
Thank You for giving me the greatest gift of all.

For God loved the world so much that He gave His only Son so that anyone who believes in Him shall not perish but have eternal life.
John 3:16

God, this Christmas, remind me of Your gifts, including

_____

_____

_____

Show me ways to share Your love with others, especially with

_____

_____

Thank You, God, for

_____

_____

                    In Jesus' name. Amen.

Someday

Dear God, You know how I sometimes wonder
    if my brother and sister
        really care about me.
They can be so mean.
They say things that hurt me
    and make me angry.
Sometimes I find myself thinking
    how I'll show them someday.
I won't always be
    their dumb little kid sister.
I'm going to grow up
    and surprise them all.
Someday …
God, I wonder what Joseph was thinking
    when his brothers threw him into that pit
        and sold him into slavery.
Did he think about that "someday"
    when he would get even?
Maybe,
    but when that someday came,
        Joseph forgave and helped them.
I know I have to do the same thing,
    not just someday—
        but today.
Help me to be forgiving.
Help me to love my brother and sister
    as I want them to love me,
        as You love me—
    and love them too.

Be gentle and ready to forgive; never hold grudges. Remember, the Lord forgave you, so you must forgive others. Most of all, let love guide your life.
Colossians 3:13–14

God, show me how to forgive others as You forgive
me, especially

Thank You, God, for

I praise You, God, for

In Jesus' name. Amen.

I Am Special!

God, it's been hard
　　　to pray about these things.
Sometimes I've hurt so bad that
　　　there haven't been any words,
　　　　　but somehow You've understood—
　　　somehow You've made me feel better.
I still don't feel pretty.
I'm not sure I'm any smarter.
I'll probably never be popular,
　　　and sometimes I still feel
　　　　　that my family doesn't love me.
But, God, in a new and beautiful way
　　　I *know* I am special.
I don't have to be anything but me.
You made me.
You love me.
And You have a plan for my life.
I feel good about me.
I am special!

For I know the plans I have for you, says the Lord. They are plans for good and not for evil, to give you a future and a hope. In those days when you pray, I will listen. You will find Me when you seek Me, if you look for Me in earnest.
Jeremiah 29:11–13

God, I need to tell You about _____
_____
_____
_____

God, thank You for answering my prayers,
especially my prayers for _____
_____
_____
_____

God, I praise You for _____
_____
_____

In my Savior's name. Amen.